Constables Dayne Campb

Criminal Desserts
Cops for Cancer Cookbook

Canadian Cancer Society
BRITISH COLUMBIA AND YUKON

COPS FOR CANCER

ENGAGE BOOKS / VANCOUVER

ENGAGE BOOKS

WWW.ENGAGEBOOKS.CA

AD Classic®, BC Classic® and SF Classic® are imprints of Engage Books

First edition published by Engage Books © 2009
Dayne Campbell & Carla Arial © 2009
Foreword by Don Duncan © 2009

Cover Image by Sasha S © 2009
Cover designed by A.R. Roumanis © 2009
Illustrated by Gabrielle Ng © 2009

Proofread by Genie Mata
Recipes by Janice Clancy, Kathy Campbell, and Tanya Vallis

Typeset & layout design by Annie Chen & Pearly Ma
Text set in 11/13 Adobe Caslon Pro
Recipe titles set in 18 Neutraface 2 Display
Chapter titles set in 30 Neutraface 2 Display

ISBN: 978-1-926606-24-6

NOTE: If you purchased this book without a cover you should be aware that this book is stolen property. It was reported as "unsold and destroyed" to the publisher, and neither the author nor the publisher has received any payment for this "stripped book."

All rights reserved. No part of this book may be reproduced in any form or by any electronic or mechanical means, including information storage and retrieval systems, or by any means, electronic, mechanical, photocopying, recording, scanning, or otherwise, without permission in writing from the publisher, except by a reviewer who may quote brief passages in a review.

The authors and publisher of this book assume no liability for, and are released by readers from, any injuries or damage resulting from the strict adherence to, or deviation from, the directions and/or recipes herein. All yields are approximations.

Engage Books
PO Box 4608
Main Station Terminal
349 West Georgia Street
Vancouver, BC
V6B 4A1
Canada

Criminal Desserts
Cops for Cancer Cookbook

*We would like to dedicate this book to all of the children
out there that have ever been affected by cancer*

Acknowledgments

Carla and I would like to thank the many people that have helped us reach our fundraising goals for the Canadian Cancer Society. We have had the pleasure of being involved in a number of events this year to raise money for both pediatric research and Camp Goodtimes. Both causes have opened our eyes to the many children out there that are in need of assistance.

What would a cookbook be without the recipes that make it a bestseller. We would like to say a big thank you to Janice Clancy, Kathy Campbell, and Tanya Vallis for all of their wonderful recipes. All three are cooking machines and can bake like no other.

A special thanks to Publisher Alexis Roumanis of Engage Books, Designers Annie Chen and Pearly Ma, Proofreader Genie Mata, and Illustrator Gabrielle Ng for all of their help. They provided a ton of direction and assistance. Without their help this book would have been written on napkins. Their expertise in this area was greatly appreciated.

We would also like to mention the terrific work that Camp Goodtimes staff and volunteers do on a yearly basis. The wonderful memories that they provide these children will last a long time.

Cst Dayne Campbell
Cst Carla Arial
Vancouver Police Department

CONTENTS

Acknowledgments	5
Foreword	8
Introduction	10
Note from the Authors	13

Recipes

Cakes & Pies	14
Bars & Squares	36
Candies & Treats	54
Cookies	78

Stories

Kale DenOtter	34
Kim Wright	52
Taylor Moon	76
David Bourne	92

Foreword

Thank you for purchasing the 2009 edition of the Cops for Cancer Tour de Coast Cookbook. The proceeds from the sale of these books will directly benefit children and families whose lives have been, or may be, affected by cancer. The police officers, who have provided the recipes that you will enjoy, are coming together as a team to embark upon an inspirational 900 kilometer bicycle journey this September, to raise funds and to show their unwavering support for this cause. You are now a part of this team and I congratulate you for "joining." Your participation will help to fund outstanding programs such as Camp Goodtimes, which serves children and their families who are dealing with cancer, as well as pediatric cancer research that will lead to more effective and less invasive procedures with reduced side effects both during treatment as well as later in life.

I've been a part of Cops for Cancer for over five years and I've met many children who have directly benefited from our efforts. I have also been moved by the stories told about children who are currently undergoing treatment for a newly diagnosed illness or a relapse. Through our Cops for Cancer Junior Team we have gotten to know kids who are not just cancer survivors, but "THRIVERS." Children and their families should never have to make the cancer journey alone. We are all there with them. When it comes to kids with cancer, there is no worthier cause.

As we ride through your community this year please remember our purpose and give us a big thumbs up to show your support. It really helps.

For more information and to visit the riders' personal fundraising web pages to see why each of them will make the journey this year please visit www.copsforcancer.ca.

Sincere thanks and bon appétit.

Don Duncan
Steering Committee Chair/Escort Leader
2009 Cops for Cancer Tour de Coast

Don Duncan (right) and the Team Captain, Buzz Whalen.

Introduction

WHAT IS COPS FOR CANCER?

The Canadian Cancer Society's Cops for Cancer is a partnership between the Canadian Cancer Society and police officers, RCMP and local military police from across British Columbia. Each fall, Canadian law enforcement personnel cycle a pre-designated route in their region, raising funds and awareness for pediatric cancer research and programs that support kids with cancer, such as Camp Goodtimes. Cops for Cancer began in Edmonton in 1994 and has grown to include many other Canadian cities and areas. In British Columbia, there are four Cops for Cancer Tours, including Vancouver Island, Greater Vancouver, the Fraser Valley, and in the North.

A COP WHO CARED AND MADE A DIFFERENCE

In June 1994, Sergeant Gary Goulet of the Edmonton Police Service met Lyle Jorgenson, a five-year-old boy who had cancer. Goulet requested the meeting after learning that Lyle was being ridiculed at school because of his hair loss due to chemotherapy. Goulet was so moved by the boy's story that he decided to do something. That was the beginning of the Canadian Cancer Society's Cops for Cancer campaign.

"My head was already shaved, so I asked Lyle to have his picture taken with me in a police cruiser," Goulet said.

Goulet gathered a group of Edmonton officers who were willing to shave their own heads and they joined the boy in school to show kids that being bald was cool.

Goulet's activities received plenty of media coverage, along with calls and letters from citizens touched by the officer's campaign. One letter, however, moved Goulet to do more. It came from a woman whose daughter had lost her hair during cancer treatment. She urged Goulet to continue his campaign.

Goulet contacted the Canadian Cancer Society and the head-shaving event caught on and was adopted by neighboring police forces. Then it spread across the country.

HOW DOES IT WORK?

Over the span of a week to twelve days, teams of cyclists make their way through British Columbia, stopping in select communities where riders participate in various fundraising events and speaking engagements. Each rider is paired with a child who has experienced cancer or who is living with cancer. These kids are honorary members of the Tour team and are an inspiration to the riders.

Training for Cops for Cancer begins in the Spring. In addition to a vigorous training schedule, riders are asked to raise funds before they can go on the ride. This involves asking friends and family for support, and also organizing fundraising events such as bake sales and head shaves. Join us in supporting the Tours.

HOW CAN YOU GET INVOLVED?

Talk to your local Canadian Cancer Society office to organize a school headshave, barbeque or fundraising dinner. You can help make a difference. And remember to cheer on your local rider team.

HOW YOU ARE HELPING BY BUYING THIS COOKBOOK?

The proceeds from this cookbook go to two causes within the Canadian Cancer Society—Camp Goodtimes and Pediatric Research.

Camp Goodtimes organizes camps and programs for kids, teenagers, and families living with cancer. Its goal is to create a safe and fun environment where friendships and lifelong memories can be made. Each of our programs is uniquely designed, but all of them take place in the comfortable and relaxed setting of Loon Lake in Maple Ridge.

Note from the Authors

Thank you for purchasing the Cops for Cancer Charity Cookbook. Cops for Cancer is a wonderful non-profit organization that assists in pediatric cancer research and benefits Camp Goodtimes, a camp where those children fighting cancer and survivors of cancer can forget about their battle and have the childhood they all deserve.

Constables Dayne Campbell and Carla Arial are Vancouver Police Officers and participants in the 2009 Cops for Cancer Tour De Coast. Each has been affected by cancer in different ways. In September 2009, they will embark in a nine day, 800 km plus bike ride for cancer. This ride will go through many communities on the south coast of British Columbia.

Your purchase has helped them in their goal to raise over $12,000.00 for the Canadian Cancer Society.

Thank you, and enjoy cooking!

Cst Dayne Campbell
Cst Carla Arial
Vancouver Police Department

✳ ✳ ✳ CAKES & PIES

BANANA OAT CAKE	16	GUM DROP CAKE	26
BANANA CREAM PIE	17	GRANNY SMITH APPLE PIE	27
CARAMEL PECAN CHEESECAKE	18	IMPOSSIBLE PIE CHERRY SLICE	27
CARNIVAL ICE CREAM CAKE	19	JELLY ROLL	28
CHOCOLATE CARROT CAKE	20	PINA COLADA CAKE	29
COOKIES & CREAM CAKE	21	LEMON MERINGUE PIE	30
COCOA PEANUT BUTTER CAKE	22	LEMON MERINGUE TARTS	30
CREAM PUFFS (CHOUX PASTRY)	23	MOCHA CHEESECAKE	31
CHOCOLATE MAYONNAISE CAKE	24	PEPPERMINT CHOCOLATE MOUSSE	32
DIXIE PIE	24	SOUR CREAM RHUBARB PIE	32
GRANDMA SHEPHERD'S VINATERTA	25	15 LAYER JELLO MOLD	33

BANANA OAT CAKE

2 cups	flour
1 cup	rolled oats
2 tsp	baking powder
1 tsp	baking soda
1 tsp	salt
½ cup	shortening
1¼ cup	sugar
2	eggs
1½ tsp	vanilla extract
1 cup	mashed banana, ripe
¾ cup	buttermilk
	or sourmilk (just add 1 tbsp of vinegar to normal milk)

Banana Icing

½ cup	butter, softened
½ cup	mashed banana
4 cups	icing sugar
1 tbsp	lemon juice
1 tsp	vanilla

COMBINE first 5 dry ingredients. Stir well to blend. Cream shortening, sugar, eggs, and vanilla together. Beat at medium speed until light and fluffy. Add dry ingredients to creamed mixture. Alternate with mashed banana and milk. Spread in greased 13 × 9 inch pan. Bake at 350°F for 35–40 mins.

To make banana icing, cream butter, mashed bananas and half the icing sugar together until light. Add lemon juice and vanilla. Gradually blend in remaining icing sugar and beating until smooth.

BANANA CREAM PIE

1	pre-baked pie shell
¾ cup	white sugar
3 tbsp	cornstarch
¼ tsp	salt
2 cups	milk
3	eggs, slightly beaten
tbsp	butter
1½ tsp	vanilla extract
4	bananas
4	egg whites
6 tbsp	white sugar

In medium sized pot, put the ¾ cup of sugar, cornstarch and salt. Whisk in milk until smooth and cook over medium heat until bubbly. Cook 2 more minutes. Stir some of the hot mixture into the egg yolk and whisk thoroughly. Pour egg mixture back into the pot; continue cooking until thickened, stirring constantly. Remove from heat and stir in the butter and vanilla.

Slice the bananas into the pie shell, cover with the filling. Beat the egg whites until foamy, slowly beat in 6 tbsp sugar until stiff peaks form. Spread on the filling, getting right to the edge. Bake at 350°F for about 12 minutes or until meringue is golden brown.

CARAMEL PECAN CHEESECAKE

2 cups	pecans, finely ground
¼ cup	sugar
¼ cup	melted butter
26	caramels
1½ tbsp	condensed milk
4 pkgs	cream cheese, room temperature (8 oz)
1 cup	sugar
3	eggs, large
1 tbsp	vanilla
1 cup	whipping cream
2 tbsp	icing sugar
½ tsp	vanilla extract

Mix first 3 ingredients together and press into springform pan. In saucepan, melt the caramels and sweetened condensed milk over low heat and drizzle over the crust. Cream the cream cheese and 1 cup sugar until fluffy. Add eggs, one at a time, beating after each addition. Stir in vanilla and pour over caramel.

Bake at 325°F for about 1 hour until set. Cool and remove the sides. Put in fridge overnight. Beat the whipping cream, icing sugar and ½ tsp, vanilla until stiff and spread on cake.

CARNIVAL ICE CREAM CAKE

1	10-inch angel food cake, baked & cooled
1 envelope	Strawberry Kool-Aid
1 envelope	Orange Kool-Aid
1 envelope	Raspberry Kool-Aid
1 pkg	frozen sliced strawberries, thawed (10 oz)
½ gallon	vanilla ice cream, slightly softened
1 pkg	frozen peaches, thawed, diced (10 oz)
1 pkg	frozen raspberries, thawed (10 oz)

TEAR the cake into bite-sized pieces and divide amongst 3 bowls. Sprinkle strawberry Kool-Aid over 1 bowl, orange over another and raspberry over the third. Toss each bowl so that the cake pieces are coated with the Kool-Aid.

LINE a tube pan with aluminum foil. Place strawberry cake pieces in pan; spoon over the strawberries with their liquid onto the cake pieces. Spread ⅓ of the ice cream over the strawberries. Repeat layers with the orange cake pieces, peaches (with their liquid), half of the remaining ice cream, the raspberry cake pieces, raspberries with their juice and remaining ice cream.

COVER and freeze for 24 hours. About 2 hours before serving, place cake in the fridge. About 30 minutes before serving, unmold on chilled plate; remove aluminum foil. Refrigerate until serving time.

CHOCOLATE CARROT CAKE

4	eggs, room temperature
2 cups	sugar
1 cup	oil
4	unsweetened chocolate squares, melted
2 cups	flour
2 tsp	baking powder
1 tsp	baking soda
½ tsp	salt
1 tbsp	cinnamon
¼ tsp	nutmeg
pinch	cloves
2 cups	carrots, grated
1 can	crushed pineapple, well drained (19 oz)
1 tsp	vanilla extract
½ cup	walnuts, chopped (optional)

Chocolate Cream Cheese Icing

6 oz	chopped semi-sweet chocolate squares
3 tbsp	water
1 pkg	cream cheese (250 g)
1 tsp	vanilla
1½ cups	icing sugar

In large bowl, beat the eggs until frothy. Gradually add the sugar, oil and melted chocolate, beating until light. Mix the flour, baking powder, baking soda, salt and spices. Beat into the egg mixture. Combine the carrots, pineapple, vanilla and nuts. Add to the batter and mix thoroughly. Pour into a greased and floured tube pan. Bake at 350°F for about 60 minutes or until toothpick inserted in center comes out clean. Invert and cool. Ice with Chocolate Cream Cheese Icing.

To make icing, melt the chocolate in the water in the microwave on low power stirring often and then cool. Beat the cream cheese, cooled chocolate and vanilla until well blended. Beat in icing sugar until fluffy.

COOKIES & CREAM CAKE

1 box	white cake mix (double-layer size)
1¼ cup	water
⅓ cup	oil
3	egg whites
1 cup	Oreo cookies, coarsely ground
2 squares	semi-sweet chocolate, melted

Creamy White Frosting

1 cup	shortening
1 tbsp	vanilla
2 cups	icing sugar
3–4 tbsp	milk

Garnish
miniature Oreos

PREPARE cake mix according to directions using water, oil and egg whites. Fold in the crushed cookies. Pour batter into two greased and floured 9 inch round cake pans. Bake at 350°F for about 30 minutes or until done. Cool in pans for 10 minutes. Remove from pans and cool completely on wire racks. Frost with Creamy White Frosting. Drizzle the melted chocolate around the top edges and garnish with miniature Oreos.

To make frosting, beat shortening and vanilla until well creamed. Gradually beat in 2 cups icing sugar and 3–4 tbsp milk to make a spreadable frosting.

COCOA PEANUT BUTTER CAKE

1 box	white cake mix (double-layer size)
½ cup	brown sugar
1¼ cup	water
¼ cup	cocoa powder
2 tbsp	icing sugar
2 tbsp	butter, softened
2 tbsp	hot water
1 cup	peanut butter chips
1 tbsp	shortening
3	eggs

Combine the cocoa, icing sugar, butter and 2 tbsp hot water in small bowl until smooth; set aside. Melt peanut butter chips and shortening on top of double boiler over hot, not boiling, water set aside.

Mix the dry cake mix, brown sugar, 1¼ cup water, eggs and melted peanut butter chip mixture in large bowl; beat until smooth. Add 1½ cups of the batter to the reserved cocoa mixture; blend well. Pour remaining batter into greased 13 × 9 inch pan; spoon dollops of the chocolate batter on top and swirl with a knife. Bake at 350°F for about 40–45 minutes until cake tester comes out clean.

CREAM PUFFS (CHOUX PASTRY)

  1 cup   boiling water
  ½ cup   butter
  1 cup   flour
  3–4   eggs

Filling
sweetened whipping cream

PLACE boiling water in saucepan; add butter and melt on medium heat. When butter is melted and while mixture is still boiling, add flour, all at once. Stir rapidly until mixture makes a ball that comes away from the sides of the pan. DO NOT OVERCOOK.

REMOVE from heat. Add unbeaten eggs, one at a time, beating each one in thoroughly before adding the next. Add the fourth egg only if mixture is not smooth enough. The secret of tender cream puffs is long and patient beating. A good rule is to beat the batter until you can cut through it with a clean knife without anything sticking to the blade.

FOR large puffs, drop by the tablespoon and for small puffs use a teaspoon. Drop on greased cookie sheet a few inches apart and twirl slightly to give a peaked effect. Bake at 400°F for 30 minutes; reduce heat to 325°F and continue baking until puffs are dry, about 10–15 minutes for small ones and 20–25 minutes for large ones.

SLIT each puff with a sharp knife in one of the natural divisions made by the expanding dough; let cool on racks before filling. Cut the tops off, scoop out any soft insides and fill with sweetened whipped cream and replace tops. You can use any filling you like. Small puffs are good with a salmon filling or anything else in that line.

CHOCOLATE MAYONNAISE CAKE

2 cups	flour
4 tbsp	cocoa
½ tsp	salt
2 tsp	baking soda
1 cup	sugar
1 cup	mayonnaise
1 cup	water
1 tsp	vanilla

BEAT everything together until smooth and pour into a greased 9 × 13 inch pan. Bake at 350°F for about 30–40 minutes until done.

DIXIE PIE

2	9-inch pie shells, partially baked
1½ cups	raisins
1 cup	butter, softened
1 cup	white sugar
1 cup	brown sugar
6	eggs
2 tsp	vanilla
2–4 tsp	cinnamon
1 cup	walnuts, chopped
1 cup	coconut, shredded

PUT raisins in small pot, just cover with water. Bring to the boil, remove from heat and set aside. Cream the butter, white sugar and brown sugar together. Beat in the eggs, vanilla and cinnamon. Drain liquid off the raisins and discard the liquid. Fold the raisins, walnuts and coconut into the egg mixture and divide between the 2 pie shells. Bake at 350°F for about 35 minutes or until set.

GRANDMA SHEPHERD'S VINATERTA

½ cup	shortening
½ cup	butter
3 tbsp	milk
3 tsp	baking powder
3½ cups	flour
1½ cups	white sugar
3	eggs
1 ½ tsp	vanilla
½ tsp	salt
½ cup	cooked dried prunes, drained
1 tsp	cinnamon
¾ cup	brown sugar
1 tsp	vanilla extract

Cream butter, shortening, white sugar, eggs, milk and 1½ tsp vanilla. Add the flour, baking powder and salt and mix well. Chill well and then roll out on lightly floured board. Cut into large cookies measuring about 7 inches in diameter. Bake on greased sheets at 350°F for about 10–12 minutes. You should have at least 5 large cookies. Cool.

Put the prunes through food chopper and put in pot with the brown sugar and cinnamon. Cook over medium heat until the sugar is dissolved and mixture is slightly thickened. Remove from heat and add 1 tsp vanilla. Cool slightly.

To assemble cake, start with a cookie on a large plate. Spread some of the prune filling on the cookie and top with another cookie, spread more prune filling on this cookie and top with another one. Keep going this way making sure that you end up with a cookie on the very top. Wrap in foil and then saran wrap and let ripen for at least 24 hours. Then ice with a thin butter icing and cut into small fingers to serve.

This is also known as Icelandic Cake.

GUM DROP CAKE

½ cup	shortening
1 cup	sugar
1	egg
½ tsp	vanilla extract
¾ cup	smooth sweetened applesauce
½ cup	hot water
2¼ cup	flour
½ tsp	baking soda
½ tsp	salt
½ tsp	cinnamon
⅛ tsp	nutmeg
⅛ tsp	ground cloves
1½ cup	raisins
½ pound	gum drops (omit black ones)
1 cup	chopped nuts

CREAM shortening. Add sugar gradually beat until light and fluffy. Add egg and vanilla beat well. Stir in applesauce and hot water. Sift together flour, soda, salt, and spices. Reserve ¼ cup of this flour mixture. Add dry ingredients to batter mix well. Fold in raisins, gumdrops, and nuts. Pour into greased 9 × 5 inch loaf pan. Bake at 300°F for 1½ hrs.

GRANNY SMITH APPLE PIE

2	unbaked pie shells
8	Granny Smith apples, large
1 cup	white sugar
1 tbsp	flour
2 tsp	cinnamon
2 tbsp	butter

Mix the apples, white sugar, flour and cinnamon together. Toss to mix well and put in pie shell. Dot with butter and cover with the other pie shell. Cut slits in top and bake at 400°F for about 60 minutes.

Note: You can use unbaked pie shells from the store, or if making your own, prepare enough dough for a double-crust pie.

IMPOSSIBLE PIE

4	eggs
1 cup	sugar
½ cup	butter
1 cup	coconut
½ cup	flour
2 cups	milk
2 tsp	vanilla
pinch	nutmeg (optional)

Mix all thoroughly by hand or in blender. Pour into greased 10-inch pie plate. Bake at 350°F for 1 hour until center is firm. The flour will settle for crust, while coconut forms topping. The centre is an egg custard filling.

JELLY ROLL

1 cup	flour
2 tsp	baking powder
¼ tsp	salt
3	egg yolks
3	egg whites
¾ cup	sugar
1 tbsp	lemon juice
1 tbsp	water

Stir the flour, baking powder and salt together and set aside. In a bowl, beat the egg yolks until thick and pale yellow; gradually beat in the sugar. Stir in the lemon juice and water. Fold in the dry ingredients, gradually. In a glass bowl, beat the egg whites until stiff but not dry; fold into the batter. Spread batter evenly on a greased and parchment lined shallow 15 × 10½ × ¾ inch pan. Bake at 325°F for about 12–15 minutes or until lightly browned and top springs back when touched.

Lay a tea towel out on counter and cover with icing sugar. As soon as cake is done, invert immediately onto the tea towel. Remove paper carefully and quickly trim off side crusts. Spread thinly with softened jelly and roll lengthwise. Wrap in cloth or wax paper, working very quickly so that the cake will not crack.

PINA COLADA CAKE

1 box	yellow cake mix (18.5 oz)
1 box	instant vanilla pudding mix (small)
1 can	coconut cream (15 oz)
½ cup	rum
2 tbsp	rum
⅓ cup	oil
4	eggs
1 can	crushed pineapple, well drained (18 oz)

Coconut Cream Sauce

1 cup	unwhipped whipping cream
½ cup	coconut cream

Garnish

pineapple chunks, well drained
maraschino cherries, well drained
toasted coconut

In a large bowl, mix the cake mix, pudding mix, ½ cup coconut cream, ½ cup rum, oil and eggs. Beat until well blended. Stir in the crushed pineapple. Pour into a well greased and floured 10-inch tube pan. Bake for 50–55 minutes or until tests done. Cool 10 minutes. Remove from pan. Poke holes all over the top of the cake about 1 inch apart almost all the way to the bottom.

Mix the remaining coconut cream and remaining rum. Slowly spoon over cake. Chill thoroughly. Garnish with pineapple chunks, maraschino cherries and toasted coconut. Serve with Coconut Cream Sauce. To make sauce, beat whipping cream and coconut cream together until just stiff.

LEMON MERINGUE PIE

1 cup	white sugar
2 tbsp	flour
3 tbsp	cornstarch
¼ tsp	salt
1½ cups	water
3	lemons, peeled & juiced
4	egg yolks, slightly beaten
4	egg whites
6 tbsp	sugar
¼ cup	butter
1	pre-baked pie shell

In large pot, mix the 1 cup white sugar, flour, cornstarch and salt. Whisk in the water and lemon juice (add more if you desire). Cook over medium heat stirring constantly until mixture boils. Turn down heat to low. Add ½ cup hot mixture into the egg yolks beating well. Add back to the pot, bring to the boil and cook until thickened stirring continually. Stir in the butter and pour into pie shell.

Beat the egg whites until foamy, slowly beat in 6 tbsp sugar and beat until stiff peaks form. Spread over the fillings, making sure you get right to the edge. Bake at 350°F for about 10–15 minutes until meringue is golden.

LEMON MERINGUE TARTS

1 envelope	meringue pie filling mix
2 dozen	pre-baked tart shells (regular size)

Prepare pie filling as per directions. Fill the cooked tart shells about ⅔ full and place them on cookie sheets. Make meringue as per directions and place some on the top of each tart. Bake at 375°F until meringue is golden.

MOCHA CHEESECAKE

1½ cups	chocolate wafers, finely chopped
1/3 cup	butter
1 tbsp	sugar

Filling

2 squares	sweet chocolate (10 oz each)
dash	salt
2 pkgs	cream cheese (8 oz each)
4	eggs
¾ cup	sugar
2–3 tsp	instant coffee

Garnish

chocolate cookies
mint leaves

COMBINE wafer crumbs, butter, and sugar. Butter sides and bottom of a 8-inch spring form pan. Press crumb mixture evenly into bottom of pan.

MELT chocolate over hot but not boiling water. Stir until smooth. Beat cream cheese until soft and smooth. Add eggs one at a time to cream cheese. Gradually add sugar, mixing well until blended. Add melted chocolate, instant coffee and salt. Stir until blended.

TURN mixture in prepared pan. Bake cake 350°F in centre of oven for approximately 40 minutes or until cake centre is almost set. It will firm up when chilled. Let cheese cake cool for 45 minutes. Cover and chill overnight.

ADD garnish.

PEPPERMINT CHOCOLATE MOUSSE

9 oz	bittersweet chocolate, chopped
¾ cup	mini marshmallows
4	egg yolks
4	egg whites
½ pint	whipping cream
dash	peppermint extract

MELT chocolate in microwave, stirring occasionally until chocolate melts. Stir the mini marshmallows into the chocolate, stirring until melted. Cool slightly, add egg yolks and stir well. Beat the egg whites until stiff and fold into the chocolate mixture. Beat the whipping cream until stiff and fold into the chocolate mixture. Stir in peppermint flavoring to taste. Chill 3 hours before serving.

SOUR CREAM RHUBARB PIE

4 cups	rhubarb, sliced
1½ cups	white sugar
1/3 cup	flour
1 cup	sour cream
1	unbaked pie shell
½ cup	flour
½ cup	brown sugar
¼ cup	butter

IN large bowl, mix the rhubarb, white sugar and ⅓ cup of flour. Mix to coat all the rhubarb and then stir in the sour cream. Pour into an unbaked pie shell. Mix the ½ cup flour, brown sugar and ¼ cup butter until crumbly. Sprinkle on the rhubarb mixture. Bake at 425°F for about 10 minutes and then lower heat to 350°F and bake for another 30 minutes or until rhubarb is cooked.

15 LAYER JELLO MOLD

1 box	red Jello (small box)
1 box	yellow Jello (small box)
1 box	orange Jello (small box)
1 box	green Jello (small box)
1¼ cups	sugar
16 oz	whipping cream
16 oz	sour cream
2 envelopes	unflavored gelatin, softened in ½ cup cold water

BRING sugar and whipping cream to a boil; add the unflavored gelatin mixture. Cool. Add sour cream. Dissolve red Jello in 1½ cup boiling water. Coat a 12-cup mold with an oil-based cooking spray like Pam. Put ¾ cup red Jello in the mold and put in fridge until set. Top with ⅔ cup cream mixture, put in fridge until set. Alternate different colors of Jello and the cream mixture.

NOTE: Make the second and third Jello mixtures a little ahead and let them cool off a little; then they will set faster. Instead of pouring the mixture into the mold, spoon on each new layer so it doesn't spoil the previous layer. If the cream mixture gets lumpy, it can be softened over a pan of warm water. If your Jello happens to thicken before you use it, set your bowl into a little hot water and stir until it is liquid again.

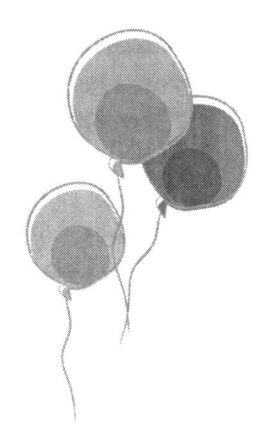

Kale DenOtter

Camp Goodtimes. How do I start with a place that has changed my life and shaped me into who I am today? This is where I have created friendships and memories more valuable than all the diamonds, gold and cold, hard cash this world holds. I pulled up to camp, on the shores of Shawnigan Lake, for the first time in 1999. It was Week 1 of camp that year, and, of course, it was also my first week at camp. When I pulled up in my mom's car, a wide-eyed seven year old, I had no idea that this would become my favourite place on earth with some of my favourite people on earth.

After that year, camp became a yearly event for me and I began to regularly attend Week Two of camp. There I have met so many people with whom I have shared amazing experiences, laughter, tears and of course hugs. I have had Skips who have given me wisdom, ideas, and helped with so many of my problems whether they be with cancer, school or with family and friends. These are people who I have looked up to and continue to look up to as teachers and mentors, and of course as just amazing friends. I have had fellow campers with whom we have shared our stories about our cancer treatment. We would share stories when we were little about how each needle or poke would hurt, and now that we are older, and maybe a little wiser, we share stories on how our treatment has affected our daily lives and our relationships with the people around us. For us older campers, (especially me) that is one reason why camp is so amazing; we get to share with kids our age exactly what we went through. For those who will be attending the Camp and the Teen Programme for the first time, if my experience is any indication, yours will be amazing, too.

And, of course, with Skips and fellow campers I have had so much FUN! Camp holds so many activities for everyone and I have amazing memories of all of them. Whether it be hanging out at arts and crafts with Nikki and Ali making bracelets, or playing soccer on the field with Aaron and Emily, or going kayaking with Cam and Drew, or just jamming on my guitar with Maleek and Mina, camp is a magical place. The opportunities to relax and talk about anything and everything with Kaiser and Kimball, or to just hanging out with Gary, Sarah and Taylor and the kind of things that make camp so cool. And of course, Silent Football (anyone who sees me at camp, I will gladly teach and play with you).

Camp Goodtimes has given me so many special experiences, be it the opening and closing ceremonies, rest and tuck, the dance, the water front, and the sleep out to name a few. For potential campers, survivors and siblings alike, this place is waiting for you to join it and begin to make your own amazing and special memories like the ones I have. I am truly blessed to have been a part of camp for the past ten years and I hope my blessing continues for many more years to come. Walt Disney has nothing on Camp Goodtimes; it is truly the greatest place on Earth.

Kale (left) & his friends, Sarah and Cam

✶ ✸ ✶ BARS & SQUARES

ALMOND BARS 1	38
ALMOND BARS 2	38
BLACK AND WHITE BARS	39
BUTTERTART SQUARES	40
BUTTERSCOTCH COCONUT SQUARES	41
CARIBBEAN BARS	42
CHOCOLATE BUTTERSCOTCH BARS	43
CHOCOLATE CHIP BARS 1	44
CHOCOLATE CHIP BARS 2	44
CHOCOLATE CHIP NOUGAT BAR	45
CHOCOLATE REVEL BARS	46
EAT MORE BARS	46
GORP BARS	47
ICED TOFFEE SQUARES	48
IRISH BARS	49
MARS BARS SQUARES	49
MARSHMALLOW DREAM SQUARES	50
MATRIMONIAL SQUARES	50
MYSTERY SQUARES	51

ALMOND BARS 1

1 cup	butter
2 cups	flour
½ cup	water
1 cup	sugar
2	eggs
1 cup	almond paste
½ tsp	vanilla extract

Cut the butter into the flour until it resembles coarse crumbs, stir in water and mix well. Divide dough in half. Take one half and roll out on floured board until it measures about 14 × 10 inches. Place in the bottom and up the sides of an ungreased 13 × 9 × 2 inch pan. Beat the sugar, eggs, vanilla and almond paste together. Pour on top of base. Roll out the other half of the dough and place on top of the almond paste mixture. Bake at 400°F for 30–35 minutes.

ALMOND BARS 2

½ cup	butter
2 tbsp	butter
6 tbsp	white sugar
1½ cups	flour
½ cup	whipping cream
½ cup	almonds, ground
1 tbsp	brown sugar
1 tsp	cinnamon
1	egg yolk, beaten

Mix first 4 ingredients together until crumbly and press into an 8 × 8 inch pan. Bake at 325°F for 20 minutes and cool. Whip cream until stiff. Fold in almonds, sugar, cinnamon and egg yolk. Spread over cooled bottom layer. Bake at 325°F for about 40 minutes. Cool and glaze with ½ cup icing sugar mixed with one tbsp lemon juice.

BLACK AND WHITE BARS

½ cup	butter
¼ cup	sugar
6 tbsp	cocoa
1 tsp	vanilla extract
1	egg, slightly beaten
2 cups	graham wafer crumbs
1 cup	coconut
½ cup	walnuts, finely chopped
3 squares	semi sweet chocolate
1 tbsp	butter

Butter Filling

½ cup	softened margarine
2 tbsp	vanilla pudding powder (not the instant kind)
3 tbsp	milk
2 cups	icing sugar

In the top of a double boiler, combine the ½ cup butter, sugar, cocoa and vanilla. Cook over hot but not boiling water, stirring constantly until smooth. Add egg; cook for 5 minutes, stirring constantly. Stir in crumbs, coconut and nuts. Press into a greased 9-inch square pan. Cool and spread with Butter Filling. Chill about 15 minutes. Melt 3 squares of chocolate with the 1 tbsp of butter and spread over top of filling.

To make filling, cream margarine until light and fluffy. Blend in pudding and milk. Gradually beat in icing sugar and beat until smooth.

BUTTERTART SQUARES

¾ cup	flour
⅓ cup	brown sugar
⅓ cup	butter
2	eggs, beaten
2 tbsp	melted butter, cooled
½ cup	white sugar
3 tbsp	flour
⅛ tsp	salt
1 tsp	vanilla
¾ cups	raisins,
1 cup	walnuts, chopped (optional)

COVER raisins with boiling water, soak for 10 minutes, drain and pat dry. Combine the ¾ cup flour, brown sugar and ⅓ cup butter until crumbly. Press into a greased 9 × 9 inch pan. Bake about 5 minutes at 350°F. Beat eggs, melted butter, white sugar, 3 tbsp flour, salt and vanilla. Add raisins and walnuts; stir. Pour mixture over the base. Return to oven for about 30 minutes or until golden brown.

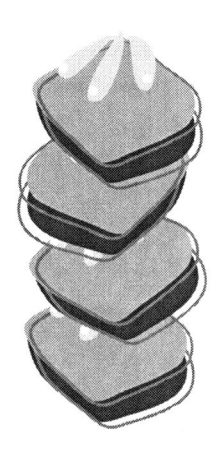

BUTTERSCOTCH COCONUT SQUARES

¼ cup	butter
½ cup	butterscotch chips
1 tsp	vanilla extract
1	egg
¼ tsp	salt
1 cup	coconut
½ cup	walnuts, chopped
2 cups	graham wafer crumbs

Custard Icing

2 tbsp	margarine
1 cup	butterscotch chips
1 cup	icing sugar
1 tbsp	custard powder
½ tsp	vanilla
4 tsp	milk

MELT butter and butterscotch chips over low heat. Add the rest of the ingredients. Stir well and pack into a greased 9 × 9 inch pan. Frost with Custard Icing.

To make icing, melt margarine and butterscotch chips, stirring until all the chips have melted. Cool slightly then beat everything together. You can add more icing sugar if necessary to make it stiffer.

CARIBBEAN BARS

½ cup	butter
¼ cup	white sugar
1¼ cups	flour
2	eggs
1 cup	brown sugar
½ cup	crushed pineapple, drain & save juice
1 cup	coconut
⅓ cup	glacé cherries, chopped
1 tsp	rum flavoring
2 tbsp	flour
½ tsp	baking powder

Mix butter, white sugar and 1¼ cups flour together until crumbly. Press into an ungreased 9 × 9 pan and bake at 350°F for 15 minutes. Beat eggs slightly; stir in remaining ingredients and spread over bottom layer. Bake at 350°F for 30 minutes or until set. Mix 1½ cups icing sugar, 3 tbsp butter, ½ tsp rum flavoring and 5 tsp of pineapple juice to make icing of spreading consistency and spread on cooled bars.

CHOCOLATE BUTTERSCOTCH BARS

1 pkg	butterscotch chips (300 g)
1 can	condensed milk (300 ml)
2 tbsp	butter
2¼ cups	brown sugar
2	eggs
1 cup	melted butter
1½ tsp	vanilla extract
1½ cups	flour
⅔ cup	oats
⅓ cup	cocoa powder
1 cup	walnuts, chopped

Heat the butterscotch chips, condensed milk and 2 tbsp butter in pan over low heat, stirring constantly until melted. Set aside. Mix brown sugar, eggs, 1 cup melted butter and vanilla; beat until smooth. Stir in the remaining ingredients and mix well.

Spread half of the dough in a greased 13 × 9 inch pan. Spread the butterscotch chip mixture evenly over the dough. Dot spoonfuls of remaining dough on top and spread lightly with knife to cover filling. Bake at 350°F for about 30–35 minutes.

CHOCOLATE CHIP BARS 1

2½ cups	flour
1/4 tsp	baking soda
1 tsp	baking powder
1½ cup	brown sugar
4 tbsp	milk
2 cups	chocolate chips
1 cup	butter
2	eggs
2 tsp	vanilla

CREAM butter and sugar until fluffy. Add milk, eggs and vanilla beating well. Add the dry ingredients – mix well. Fold in the chocolate chips and pour into a greased 9 × 13 pan. Bake at 350°F for about 30 minutes.

CHOCOLATE CHIP BARS 2

4	eggs, well beaten
2 cups	chocolate chips
1 cup	brown sugar
2 cups	flour
2 tsp	baking soda
2 cups	brown sugar
½ cup	butter
1 cup	oats, 1 cup
2 tsp	vanilla extract
½ cup	melted butter
2 tbsp	flour

COMBINE 2 cups flour and ½ cup butter until crumbly. Mix in 2 cups of brown sugar, baking soda and oats. Press into a greased 9 × 13 pan. Beat together the eggs, chocolate chips, 1 cup brown sugar, ½ cup melted butter, 2 tbsp flour and vanilla. Pour over the base and bake at 350°F for about 35 minutes.

CHOCOLATE CHIP NOUGAT BAR

1 cup	sugar
⅔ cup	light corn syrup
2 tbsp	water
2	egg whites (or ¼ cup), room temperature
2 cups	sugar
1¼ cup	light corn syrup
¼ cup	melted butter
2 tsp	vanilla
2 cups	walnuts, finely chopped
1 cup	mini chocolate chips

Line a 15½ × 10½ × 1 inch jelly pan with aluminum foil; grease foil well. Set aside. Combine the 1 cup sugar, ⅔ cup corn syrup and the water in small heavy saucepan. Cook over medium heat, stirring constantly, until sugar dissolves. Continue cooking without stirring. When mixture reaches 230°F on candy thermometer or Thread Stage (see cold water test in Candies & Treats), start beating egg whites in large glass bowl; beat until stiff, but not dry. When syrup reaches Soft Ball Stage or 238°F remove from heat.

Pour hot syrup in a thin stream over beaten egg whites, beating constantly on high speed. Continue beating 4 or 5 minutes or until mixture becomes very thick. Cover and set aside.

Combine 2 cups sugar and 1¼ cup corn syrup in heavy 2-quart saucepan. Cook over medium heat, stirring constantly, until sugar dissolves. Cook, without stirring, until it reaches the Soft Crack Stage or 275°F. Pour hot syrup all at once over reserved egg white mixture; blend with wooden spoon.

Stir in the melted butter and vanilla; stir in the nuts and mix thoroughly. Pour into prepared pan. Sprinkle evenly with mini chocolate chips and let set overnight. Cut into square and store, covered, in cool, dry place.

CHOCOLATE REVEL BARS

3 cups	oatmeal
1 tsp	baking soda
2 cups	brown sugar
2½ cups	flour
1 cup	butter
2	eggs
2 tsp	vanilla extract
1½ cups	chocolate chips
1 can	condensed milk (300 ml)

Stir together oatmeal, flour, baking soda and 1 tsp salt. In a different bowl, beat 1 cup butter and brown sugar until fluffy. Add eggs and vanilla and beat well. Mix in the oatmeal mixture. In a heavy saucepan melt the chocolate chips, sweetened condensed milk, 2 tbsp Butter and ½ tsp salt over low heat until smooth. Remove from heat. Put two-thirds of the oatmeal mixture in an ungreased 15 × 10 × 1 inch pan and press in firmly. Spread the chocolate mixture on top and sprinkle the remaining oatmeal over. Bake at 350°F for about 30 minutes. Let cool before cutting. You can substitute chocolate chips with butterscotch chips or mint chocolate chips.

EAT MORE BARS

¾ cup	honey
1 cup	peanut butter
10	marshmallows, regular sized
1 cup	chocolate chips
1 cup	salted peanuts
3 cups	Rice Krispies

In large pot, bring honey and peanut butter to a boil over medium heat. Stirring constantly, add the 10 regular-sized marshmallows and chocolate chips stirring until melted. Remove from heat and stir in peanuts and Rice Krispies. Press into a greased 9 × 13 inch pan.

GORP BARS

2 cups	crispy corn cereal, bite-sized squares
2½ cups	thin pretzel sticks, broken in half
1½ cups	peanut M & M's
1 cup	dried banana chips, unsalted
¾ cup	golden raisins
½ cup	butter
⅓ cup	creamy peanut butter
1 bag	marshmallows (10 oz)

In a large bowl, combine the cereal, pretzels, candies, banana chips and raisins. In medium saucepan, melt the peanut butter, butter and marshmallows. Stir over low heat until smooth. Immediately pour over the cereal mixture, mixing until everything is thoroughly coated. Press lightly into a greased 13 × 9 inch pan. Let sit until firm. You can substitute dried cherries, dried blueberries or dried cranberries for the raisins. You can replace the Peanut M & M's with regular ones and add ½ cup chopped almonds, cashews or walnuts.

ICED TOFFEE SQUARES

½ cup	butter
¼ cup	white sugar
1¼ cups	flour
pinch	salt
½ cup	butter
½ cup	brown sugar
2 tbsp	corn syrup
½ cup	condensed milk
2 tbsp	butter
2 tbsp	milk
1½ cups	icing sugar
½ cup	cocoa powder
1 tsp	vanilla extract

Mix the ½ cup butter, white sugar, flour and salt together and press into a greased 9 × 9 inch pan. Bake at 350°F for about 15 minutes. Combine the ½ cup butter, brown sugar, syrup and sweetened condensed milk in saucepan. Bring to the boil and boil for 5 minutes, stirring constantly. Remove from heat. Beat and pour over bottom layer. Cool. Bring the 2 tbsp butter and 2 tablespoons milk to a boil only to melt butter. Add icing sugar, cocoa and vanilla. Beat well and spread over cooled squares. Cut into very small squares as it is very rich.

IRISH BARS

½ cup	butter, softened
1½ cups	brown sugar
1 cup	flour
1 tbsp	flour
¼ tsp	salt
2	eggs
1 tbsp	Irish Mist liqueur
1 cup	nuts, chopped

In large bowl, combine the butter, ½ cup brown sugar and 1 cup flour; blend until crumbly. Press firmly into a greased 9-inch square pan. Bake at 350°F for 10 minutes; set aside to cool. In large bowl, combine 1 cup brown sugar, 1 tbsp flour and salt; blend well. Add eggs, one at a time, mixing well after each addition. Blend in liqueur and stir in nuts. Spread evenly over cooled crust. Bake at 350°F for 20 minutes. Cool in pan before slicing.

MARS BARS SQUARES

4	Mars bars
2 cups	Rice Krispies
½ cup	coconut
½ cup	butter
½ cup	chocolate chips
¼ cup	butter

Cut each Mars bar into 6 or 8 pieces. Melt with the ½ cup butter in microwave. Add Rice Krispies and coconut; mix well. Pat into greased square pan. Melt chocolate chips and ¼ cup butter in microwave; mix well and pour over Mars bar base. Refrigerate.

MARSHMALLOW DREAM SQUARES

½ pkg	graham wafer crumbs
½ cup	melted butter
¾ cup	chocolate chips
1	egg, well beaten
½ pkg	mini marshmallows
¾ cup	coconut
½ cup	brown sugar

Combine graham wafer crumbs, marshmallows, coconut and chocolate chips. Melt the butter and add brown sugar. Remove from heat and quickly stir in the egg. Add the marshmallow mixture and press into a greased 9 × 9 inch pan. Frost with butter icing and keep chilled.

MATRIMONIAL SQUARES

1½ cups	flour
1 cup	brown sugar
½ tsp	baking soda
¼ tsp	salt
1 tsp	baking powder
1½ cups	oatmeal
1 cup	butter
½ lb	dates, chopped
½ cup	cold water
1 tsp	vanilla extract

Mix the flour, sugar, baking soda, salt, baking powder and oatmeal together. Cut in the butter until crumbly. Press two-thirds of this mixture into a greased 9 × 9 inch pan and reserve the rest. Put the dates, cold water and vanilla into a saucepan and cook over medium heat until mixture is cooked and smooth. Spread over the oatmeal base and sprinkle with remaining oatmeal mixture. Bake at 325°F for about 35 minutes or until done.

MYSTERY SQUARES

1 cup	butter
2 cups	flour
½ cup	brown sugar
2	eggs, beaten
½ cup	brown sugar
2 tbsp	flour
½ tsp	baking powder
1 cup	dates, chopped
1 cup	walnuts
1½ cups	coconut

Butter Icing

½ cup	butter
2–2½ cups	icing sugar
3–4 tbsp	milk
1 tsp	vanilla

Mix first 3 ingredients together until crumbly and press into an ungreased 9 × 9 inch pan. Beat eggs slightly in bowl and add remaining ingredients. Stir until well mixed and spread over uncooked bottom layer. Bake at 350°F to 30 minutes until browned and set. Frost with Butter Icing if desired.

To making icing, beat butter until light and fluffy. Gradually add icing sugar alternating with the milk until of spreading consistency. Beat in vanilla.

Kim Wright

Camp Goodtimes holds a special place in my heart: it was here where I realized that my family could LIVE with Cancer. My son's brain tumour was diagnosed seven years ago when he was just a baby, and we'd already lived through four grueling years of hospitals, relapses, chemo and appointments by the time we first arrived, broken, at Camp Goodtimes in July of 2005.

I had not wanted to go to camp that first year. "Why would we want to be around cancer and sickness?" I said. "Haven't we had enough of that?" My husband insisted, "Let's just give it a try; if we don't like it we can come home."

I am so thankful we went. As soon as we arrived at camp, we felt embraced, like a weight was lifted from our shoulders. Ironically, it was the first time in a long time that we didn't think about cancer and sickness. Being at camp opened my eyes and my heart. I saw that my life and my family were not the only ones affected by this disease—so many families were.

And, here at Camp Goodtimes, these families seemed so brave, so fearless, despite what they were facing. They even seemed to be happy, something I had not been able to imagine before. It was a turning point for me. I came to accept that no matter what you are given to deal with in life, it's how you deal with it that counts.

Since that first summer, we've returned to the Camp Goodtimes Family Program every year. And now we are one of those happy families who have learned to face the challenge and LIVE our lives with cancer as best we can.

Kim Wright's son, Casey, with a Cops for Cancer rider

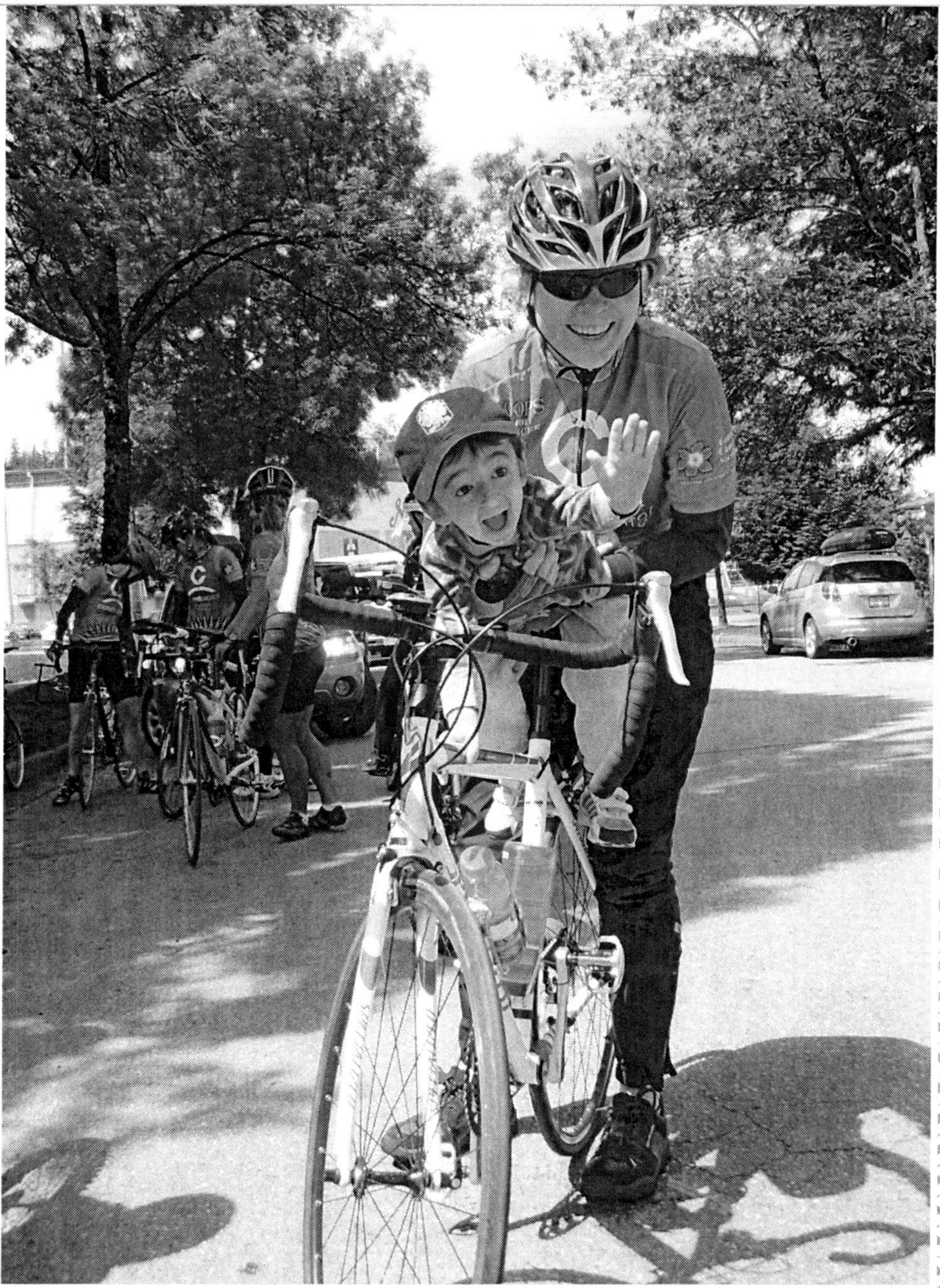

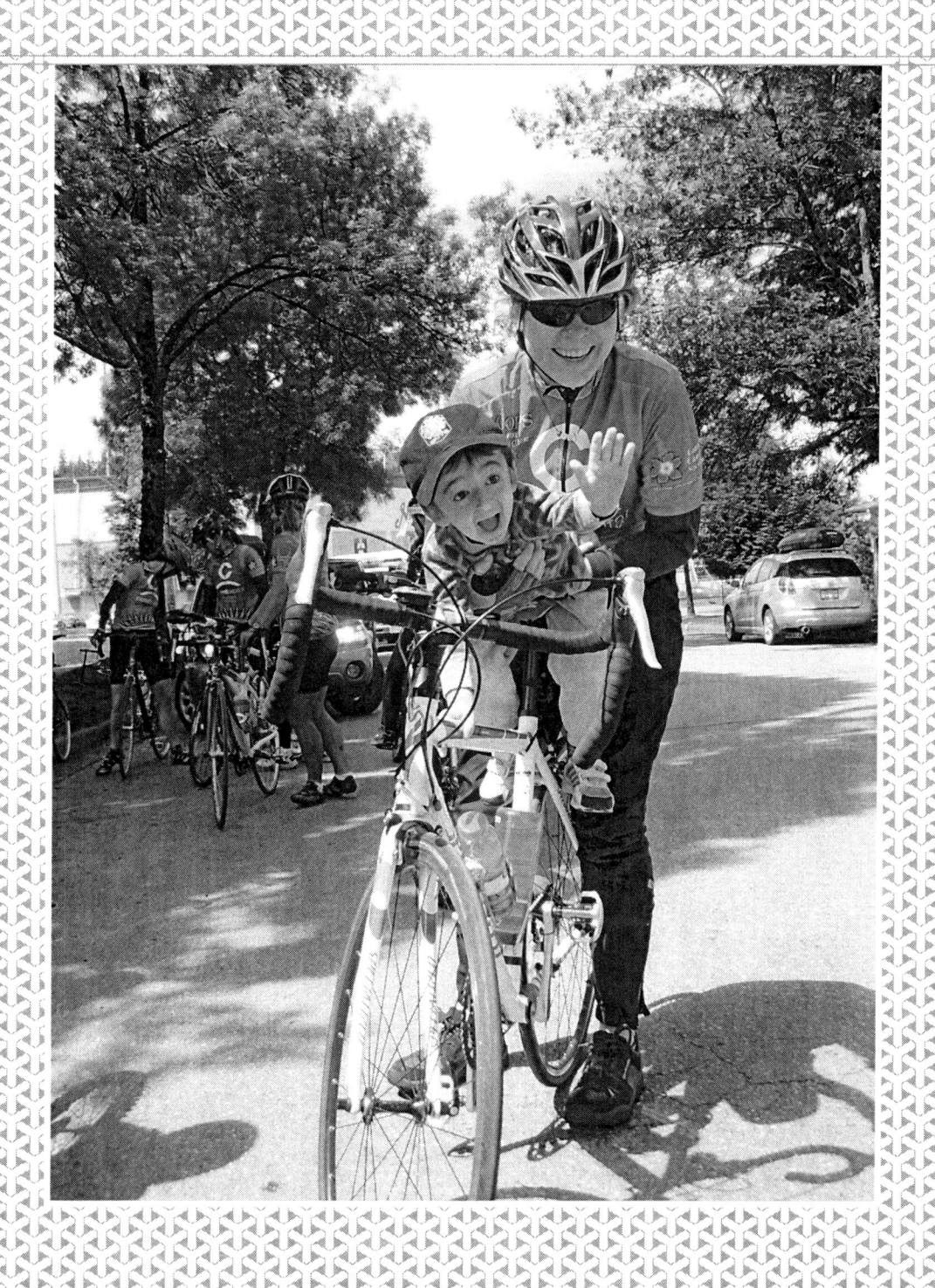

# CANDIES & TREATS

ALMOND ROCA	57	LOLLIPOPS	66
BIRD'S NEST	57	MARSHMALLOW DELIGHTS	67
APRICOT ZINGS	58	MICROWAVE PEANUT BRITTLE	67
CARAMEL FUDGE POPCORN	59	MOLASSES PULL TAFFY	68
CARAMEL POPCORN	59	POPCORN BALLS	68
CHOCOLATE CHERRY STRIPES	60	MOLASSES POPCORN MIXTURE	69
CHOCOLATE CONFETTI	61	NEVER FAIL FUDGE	70
CHOCOLATE MINT STICKS	61	NUTS & FLUFF	71
COCOA KRISPIE ROLL	62	POPPYCOCK	71
COCONUT ICE CANDY	62	PEANUT CHEW	72
CREAMY COCOA TAFFY	63	PECAN CLUSTER CRUNCH	73
DIVINITY FUDGE	64	ROCKY ROAD FUDGE	74
DIRT PUDDING CUPS	65	SWEET NUT SNACKS	74
DOUBLE CHOCOLATE FUDGE	66		

COLD WATER TEST FOR CANDY

Type of Candy	Degrees °F	Sign
thread	230 – 234	Syrup forms 2-inch thread when dropped in cold water from spoon.
soft ball	234 – 240	Syrup forms a soft ball which flattens on removal.
firm ball	244 – 248	Syrup forms a firm ball which does not flatten on removal.
hard ball	250 – 266	Syrup forms a ball hard enough to hold its shape, yet is also elastic.
soft crack	270 – 290	Syrup separates into threads which are hard but not brittle when removed from water.
hard crack	above 290	Syrup separates into threads which are hard and brittle when removed from water.

NOTE: For all tests drop a bit of the candy from a spoon into a glass of cold water and then remove. Be very careful as hot candy mixture can give you a nasty burn.

ALMOND ROCA

1 pound	butter
2 cups	white sugar
¼ tsp	cream of tartar
½ cup	toasted almonds, ground
4 tbsp	boiling water
3 squares	semi-sweet chocolate

In medium heavy pot, melt butter; add sugar, stir and bring to the boil. Add cream of tartar and boiling water and cook, stirring constantly, until it reaches 266°F on a candy thermometer or hard ball stage. Pour onto greased cookies sheet. Melt chocolate with 1 tsp. Of butter and spread on top of hardened candy and sprinkle with the almonds. Break into pieces.

BIRD'S NEST

3 tbsp	cocoa
½ cup	butter
1 tin	condensed milk
3 cups	graham wafer crumbs
1 pkg	big marshmallows
some	coconut

Mix all ingredients except marshmallows. Roll mixture around the marshmallows. Roll in coconut. Put in freezer 10 minutes then cut each marshmallow in three or four pieces.

APRICOT ZINGS

1 cup	graham wafer crumbs
1 cup	flour
1 cup	brown sugar
½ cup	coconut
½ tsp	salt
¾ cup	melted butter
1 cup	dried apricots
some	water (for covering fruit)
2	eggs
1 cup	brown sugar
1 tbsp	lemon juice
⅓ cup	flour
½ tsp	baking powder
¼ tsp	salt

COMBINE first 5 ingredients in bowl. Add melted butter and mix; reserve 1 cup. Pack the rest into an ungreased 9 × 9 inch pan and bake at 350°F for 10 minutes.

SIMMER apricots in water for 15 minutes. Drain and chop and set aside.

BEAT eggs until frothy; add lemon juice and 1 cup brown sugar. Mix well. Mix the ⅓ cup flour, baking powder and ¼ tsp. Salt into the egg mixture, stir and add apricots and stir again.

SPREAD over the bottom layer and sprinkle with reserved crumbs. Bake at 350°F for 30–35 minutes. Cool before cutting.

CARAMEL FUDGE POPCORN

1 pkg	caramels (14 oz)
2 tbsp	whipping cream
3 quarts	popped corn
1 pkg	chocolate chips (6 oz)

In a 3 quart microwaveable bowl, combine the caramels and heavy cream. Cover with lid or plastic wrap and microwave on high for 3 minutes, stirring after every minute, until mixture comes to a boil. Pour caramel sauce over popcorn, stirring to coat evenly. Quickly stir in the chocolate chips. Transfer to large cookie sheet. When cool, break into pieces.

CARAMEL POPCORN

1 cup	butter
2 cups	brown sugar
½ cup	corn syrup
6 quarts	popped popcorn
1 tsp	salt
½ tsp	baking soda
1 tsp	vanilla extract

Melt butter, add sugar, syrup and salt. Bring to the boil, stirring constantly. Boil without stirring for five minutes and remove from heat. Add the soda and vanilla and stir. Pour over the popped popcorn and mix well. Put into a large roaster and bake for about 1 hour at 225°F. Stir about every 15 minutes. Remove from oven and break apart any clumps. Store in covered containers.

CHOCOLATE CHERRY STRIPES

1 cup	butter, softened
1½ cups	sugar
2 tsp	vanilla extract
1	egg
2½ cups	flour
1½ tsp	baking powder
¾ tsp	salt
½ cup	candied cherries, finely diced
⅓ cup	walnuts, finely chopped
1 square	unsweetened baking chocolate, melted & cooled
½ cup	hot milk

In large bowl, cream the butter and sugar until smooth. Add egg and vanilla; blend well. Stir together the flour, baking powder and salt. Gradually add dry ingredients to the creamed mixture, beating well.

Divide dough into thirds. Stir cherries into ⅓ of the dough. Blend chocolate and nuts into remaining dough.

Shape the cherry dough into a 9 × ¾ inch bar. Shape the chocolate dough into a 9 × 1½ inch bar. Wrap each bar in plastic wrap and chill until firm. Cut chocolate dough in half lengthwise. Brush cut sides of the chocolate dough with hot milk. Brush both sides of the cherry dough with milk.

Place cherry dough between the two chocolate portions; press together. Wrap in plastic wrap and chill until firm. Cut into ¼ inch slices and bake on ungreased cookie sheets for about 10 minutes or until set.

CHOCOLATE CONFETTI

½ cup	peanut butter
¼ cup	butter
1 pkg	chocolate chips, small
1 bag	mini marshmallows, small & coloured

Melt butter, peanut butter and chocolate chips over medium heat, stirring constantly. Remove from heat and cool till lukewarm and add marshmallows. Stir until all the marshmallows are covered and spread into a greased 8×8 inch pan. Keep chilled.

CHOCOLATE MINT STICKS

2 oz	unsweetened chocolate squares
½ cup	butter
2	eggs
1 cup	sugar
½ cup	flour
½ tsp	peppermint flavoring
dash	salt
2 tbsp	butter
1 cup	icing sugar
1 tbsp	milk
1½ tsp	peppermint flavoring

Melt the chocolate with the ½ cup of butter. Beat eggs and sugar until fluffy. Add the chocolate mixture, ½ tsp. peppermint flavoring, flour and salt. Mix well and spread in a greased 9 × 9 pan. Bake at 350°F for about 20 minutes. Cool. Beat together the 2 tbsp. butter, milk, icing sugar and 1½ tsp peppermint flavoring and spread on the cake base.

COCOA KRISPIE ROLL

¾ cup	corn syrup
¾ cup	white sugar
¾ cup	peanut butter
2 tbsp	butter
4½ cups	Rice Krispies
⅓ cup	butter
2 tbsp	milk
1½ cup	icing sugar
⅓ cup	cocoa

Melt the corn syrup and sugar in large pot. Remove from heat and add peanut butter and 2 tbsp. butter. Add Rice Krispies and mix well. Press into a well greased wax paper lined cookie sheet. Melt ⅓ cup butter and milk over low heat. Add the icing sugar and cocoa. Beat till well mixed. Remove Rice Krispie base from pan, peel off the wax paper and spread with the icing. Roll up like a jelly roll. Wrap up in well greased wax paper and chill. Cut into thin slices.

COCONUT ICE CANDY

3 cups	white sugar
1 cup	cream
1 tsp	butter
1½ cups	coconut
1 tsp	vanilla

Put the sugar and cream in heavy saucepan on medium heat. Stirring constantly, cook until sugar is dissolved and then bring to a boil and let it boil without stirring until it forms the soft ball stage at 240°F. Remove from heat and add the butter, coconut and vanilla. Beat until creamy and pour into greased pan or drop by spoonfuls on waxed paper.

CREAMY COCOA TAFFY

1¼ cup	sugar
¾ cup	light corn syrup
⅓ cup	cocoa powder
⅛ tsp	salt
2 tsp	white vinegar
¼ cup	evaporated milk
1 tbsp	butter

GREASE a 9 inch square pan and set aside. Combine sugar, corn syrup, cocoa, salt and vinegar in heavy 2 quart saucepan.

COOK over medium heat, stirring constantly, until mixture boils; add evaporated milk and butter. Continue to cook, stirring occasionally, until it reaches the Firm Ball Stage or 248°F on a candy thermometer.

POUR mixture into pan. Let stand until cool enough to handle. Butter hands; stretch taffy, folding and pulling until light in color and hard to pull. Place taffy on table; pull into ½ inch wide strips and cut into 1 inch pieces with buttered scissors. Wrap individually in plastic wrap.

DIVINITY FUDGE

1½ cups	brown sugar
½ cup	water
1 tsp	white vinegar
1	egg white, stiffly beaten
½ tsp	vanilla extract
½ cup	nuts, chopped

In a heavy 2 quart saucepan, combine the brown sugar, water and vinegar. Cook over medium heat, stirring constantly until sugar dissolves and mixture begins to boil.

Cook to hard ball stage (250°F) without stirring. Remove from heat immediately and gradually pour over the stiffly beaten egg white, beating until thick and mixture holds its shape.

Fold in the nuts and vanilla. Drop by teaspoonfuls onto waxed paper or spread in buttered pan and cut into squares.

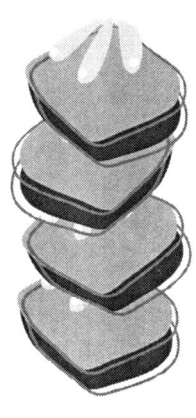

DIRT PUDDING CUPS

1 pound	cream filled chocolate cookies, crushed to fine crumbs
¼ cup	butter
1 pkg	cream cheese, softened (8 oz)
1 cup	icing sugar
1 tsp	vanilla extract
4 boxes	instant chocolate pudding mixes (small)
6 cups	milk
4⅓ cups	Cool Whip, thawed
some	gummy worms

COMBINE the butter, cream cheese, icing sugar and vanilla and beat until smooth. Add the chocolate pudding powders and milk, beat on low to combine.

FOLD the Cool Whip in and assemble in each cup the following:
1st layer–cookie crumbs;
2nd layer–pudding mixture;
3rd layer–cookies crumbs;
4th layer–pudding mixture;
5th layer–cookie crumbs.

TUCK the ends of gummy worms into the top layer so the worms are popping out of the cookie dirt.

CHILL at least 3 hours before serving. Can also make in pan and cut into squares or in large bowl.

DOUBLE CHOCOLATE FUDGE

2 squares	semi-sweet chocolate
2 cups	condensed milk
2 tsp	vanilla extract
1 cup	nuts, chopped
1 square	white chocolate

Microwave semi-sweet chocolate and 1½ cups of condensed milk in 2 quart bowl on high for 1 minute; stir well. Microwave 1 more minute; stir well. Stir until chocolate is completely melted and smooth. Stir in the vanilla and nuts. Spread into a greased 9 inch square pan. Microwave white chocolate and ½ cup sweetened condensed milk on high for 1 minute; stir well. Microwave for another 30–60 seconds until white chocolate is completely melted. Stir until smooth. Spread over the chocolate layer in the pan. Refrigerate until firm; cut into small squares.

LOLLIPOPS

2 cups	sugar
1 cup	water
1 cup	light corn syrup
optional	food coloring
¼ tsp	flavoring (use flavor oil or extracts)

Mix the sugar, water and corn syrup in a heavy pot. Cook over medium heat until the sugar dissolves. Cook on high heat, stirring constantly until it reaches about 290°F or the Soft Crack stage. Remove from heat and stir in flavoring and coloring. Pour onto greased cookie sheets into puddles. Insert popsicle sticks immediately. If desired, can sprinkle with candy sprinkles or inset candies.

MARSHMALLOW DELIGHTS

3 pkg	McIntosh toffee bar, broken up (2oz)
¼ cup	butter
⅔ cup	condensed milk
4 cups	Special K cereal
30 - 35	large marshmallows

PUT toffee pieces, butter and milk in top of double boiler. With heat on medium-hot, stir the mixture until it is melted and smooth. Remove from heat; keep toffee mixture over hot water so it doesn't set. Put the cereal into a large bowl. Stick a fork into the end of a marshmallow, dip it in the toffee, then roll in the cereal. Push off fork onto waxed paper to set.

MICROWAVE PEANUT BRITTLE

½ cup	corn syrup
1 cup	sugar
dash	salt
1 cup	peanuts
1 tsp	vanilla extract
1 tbsp	butter
1 tsp	baking soda

IN a 1 quart microwave bowl, mix the corn syrup, sugar, salt and peanuts. Turn microwave on high and cook for 7–8 minutes. Stir in the vanilla and butter. Microwave on high for another 2–3 minutes, mixture should be slightly browned. Add baking soda and stir very quickly. Turn out on lightly greased cookie sheet. Let cool and break into pieces.

MOLASSES PULL TAFFY

2 cups	white sugar
1 cup	molasses
½ cup	water
1 tbsp	vinegar
¼ tsp	cream of tartar
⅛ tsp	baking soda
2 tbsp	butter

COMBINE sugar, molasses, water and vinegar in a heavy 3 quart saucepan. Cook over medium heat, stirring constantly until sugar dissolves and mixture comes to a full boil. Add cream of tartar and cook to about 260°F or hard ball stage. Remove from heat; stir in the baking soda and butter, mixing well. Pour into shallow buttered baking dish. When cool enough to handle, pull it with the hands, until it is porous and light colored—takes about 20–30 minutes. Cut into 1 inch lengths and chill for a few minutes to harden.

POPCORN BALLS

½ cup	corn syrup
½ cup	molasses
¼ tsp	salt
1 tsp	vinegar
2 tbsp	butter
8 cups	popped corn

COMBINE syrup, molasses, salt and vinegar in a heavy 3 quart saucepan. Cook to the hard ball stage (256°F) stirring constantly to prevent burning. Remove from heat; add butter, stirring until just mixed. Slowly pour cooked syrup mixture over the popped corn, mixing well. Butter hands lightly and quickly shape mixture into balls.

MOLASSES POPCORN MIXTURE

¼ cup	butter
1½ cup	white sugar
½ cup	corn syrup
½ cup	molasses
2 tbsp	vinegar
½ tsp	salt
½ tsp	baking soda
½	walnuts, large chunks
½ cup	pecans, large chunks
½ cup	almonds, whole
½ cup	hazelnuts, large chunks
2 quarts	popped corn

In a medium, heavy saucepan, melt butter over low heat. Stir in sugar, corn syrup, molasses, vinegar and salt. Bring to the boil, stirring constantly. Reduce heat and gently boil until the mixture reaches the hard ball stage (260°F). Remove from heat, stir in baking soda and nuts. Pour over the popped corn, stirring gently to coat evenly. Transfer to large cookie sheet, let cool and break into chunks. Store in airtight container

NEVER FAIL FUDGE

2 ½ cups	sugar
¼ cup	butter
1	evaporated milk (small can)
1 jar	marshmallow cream (7 ½ oz)
¾ tsp	salt
¾ tsp	vanilla extract
1 pkg	chocolate chips (12 oz)
½ cup	walnuts, chopped

In a large saucepan, combine the first 5 ingredients. Stir over low heat until blended. Bring to a full rolling boil. Boil slowly, stirring constantly, for 5 minutes. Remove from heat, stir in vanilla and chocolate until chocolate is melted. Add nuts and pour into a greased 9 inch square pan. Cool and cut into squares.

Note: When bringing to full rolling boil, be careful not to mistake escaping air bubbles for boiling.

CANDIES & TREATS

NUTS & FLUFF

6 cups	popped popping corn
6 cups	Shreddies cereal
1 cup	salted peanuts
½ cup	butter
½ cup	smooth peanut butter
1 pkg	marshmallows (250 g)

Toss together the popcorn, cereal and peanuts. In a large microwaveable bowl, melt the butter and peanut butter together on medium-high for 1 minute. Add marshmallows and microwave for 1 more minute or until marshmallows puff. Stir in the popcorn mixture until well coated. Pour into 2 greased cookie sheets and bake at 250°F for about 10 minutes. Cool completely and break into small pieces. Store in an airtight container.

POPPYCOCK

1 cup	popcorn, unpopped
1 cup	butter
2 cups	brown sugar
3 cups	nuts
½ cup	corn syrup
½ tsp	baking soda
1 tsp	vanilla

Pop popcorn and dump into large roasting pan. In saucepan, melt butter, brown sugar and corn syrup; boil hard for 5 minutes stirring continually. Remove from heat; add vanilla and soda. Sprinkle nuts over popcorn. Pour over the brown sugar mixture. Stir. Roast in oven at 250°F for 1 hour, stirring occasionally. Break apart as it is cooling and store in airtight containers.

PEANUT CHEW

  1 cup   honey
2 cups   chocolate chips
  1 cup   peanut butter
2 cups   salted peanuts, chopped

LINE a cookie sheet with aluminum foil. If you wet your hands under water and then run your hands over the bottom and sides of the pan before you put in the foil, the foil won't slip around when you are spreading the peanut mixture in it.

COMBINE the honey and chocolate chips in a heavy saucepan. Place on low heat until the chips start to melt. Stir often.

TURN the heat to medium-high. Stir constantly until the mixture starts to boil.

REMOVE the pan from the heat and add the peanut butter. Stir until mixture becomes smooth. Add the peanuts, stir till well mixed. Spread on foil. Put in the fridge for 15 minutes, then cut. Store in a container with a lid with waxed paper between the layers.

PECAN CLUSTER CRUNCH

4 cups	Shreddies cereal
1 cup	pecans, coarsely chopped
2 tsp	cinnamon
½ cup	brown sugar
¼ cup	butter
¼ cup	corn syrup
¼ tsp	baking soda

Mix the cereal, nuts and cinnamon in large bowl. In a medium saucepan, combine the brown sugar, butter and corn syrup.

Bring to the boil, stirring constantly. Boil for 2 minutes without stirring. Stir in the baking soda.

Pour over the cereal mixture and mix until all the pieces are coated. Spread evenly on a greased cookie sheet and bake at 250°F for 30–35 minutes, stirring occasionally. Cool completely. Store in airtight container.

ROCKY ROAD FUDGE

1 ½ cups	chocolate chips
1 can	sweetened condensed milk
2 tbsp	butter
2 tsp	vanilla extract
2 cups	peanuts, salted, chopped
1 pkg	coloured mini marshmallows

On top of double boiler, melt the chocolate chips, condensed milk and butter. Remove from heat and add the vanilla and nuts. Cool till lukewarm and add the marshmallows. Spread into a 9 × 9 inch wax paper lined pan and chill.

SWEET NUT SNACKS

2 cups	mixed nuts
1	egg white, slightly beated
5 tbsp	sugar
2 - 4 tsp	cinnamon
1 cup	raisins
½ tsp	salt

Combine the nuts and egg white, mixing well so nuts are coated. If using salted nuts, omit salt. Mix the cinnamon, salt and sugar and mix into the nuts. Spread on cookie sheet and bake at 300°F for about 20 minutes. Stir once or twice. Remove add raisins and salt.

Taylor Moon

Hours, days, weeks and months have past since we were all at camp and I can't help but stop and miss it. Time passes and life happens, distances separates and we all grow up. Yet knowing and believing in camp as I do helps to remind me that, yes, time may pass but I will always be counting down to that one week where time will freeze again. For me camp is a week away from reality, where everything else stops – the chemo stops, the teasing stops and the pain stops. I can show my scars without explanation or embarrassment and laugh in knowing that we can all understand. I don't return to camp each summer to forget my past and ignore having had cancer, but simply to embrace it and give hope to those still going through it. It's seven days without the reminder that life can be short, without the needles and the 'what ifs'. No check-ups and no fear.

To me camp is about getting to be a kid again, you're able to take back that small part of your childhood where you're able to run, laugh and cry. You become accustomed to the ones singing of chicken train in 'perfect' key way too early in the morning and the constant reminders to wear your safety shoes. It's about tying together all the stupid stuff that makes camp amazing. For in the end, that week, those few days, we aren't kids missing limbs, we aren't terminally ill kids and we aren't sick kids. We are normal.

I don't have a lot of childhood memories of camp as some do but really just small clips of a place I was scared to enjoy. After having finished chemo and leaving the hospital I chose to put that part of me away, and no longer be called the cancer kid. I didn't realize what I was missing and how much returning to that place helps me to understand and cope with that other part of me. I can't not go back now, for it's become the one week in my life where I can just live. I learned a lot of things from being a camper; simple things like to take home a rock or a collection of your awards and crafts. To laugh as much as possible and to take advantages of the Skips who are willing to do anything to make you smile. I learned to cry and I learned what a real hug feels like. But for me, most importantly, I learned to live, love and laugh. So, to all of us campers, enjoy every second that you lay in your bunk awake at night worrying about the bugs biting, because you'll miss it once you're home.

Taylor (right) and her friend.

COOKIES

BUTTERSCOTCH COOKIES	80
CHOCOLATE CHIP COOKIES	81
SNOWBALLS	81
CINNAMON TREATS	82
BANANA BONANZA COOKIES	83
BOILED RAISIN COOKIES	84
MAGIC CHIPIT BAR COOKIES	85
CHERRY SURPRISES	85
CHOCOLATE SANDWICH COOKIES	86
KRACKER JACK COOKIES	87
MARILYN'S OATMEAL COOKIES	88
MONSTER COOKIES	88
COCOA PECAN KISSES	89
COCONUT FINGERS	90
COFFEE FINGERS	91

BUTTERSCOTCH COOKIES

3.4 cup	butter
½ cup	icing sugar
¼ tsp	salt
1¾ cup	flour
1 pkg	butterscotch chips (12 oz)
3.4 cup	pecans, chopped
2 cups	icing sugar
¼ cup	rum

In large bowl, cream the butter, ½ cup icing sugar and salt until light and fluffy. Gradually add flour, beating until well blended. Stir in butterscotch chips and pecans.

Drop by spoonfuls on greased cookie sheet about 1 inch apart.

Bake at 325°F for 15 minutes or until cookies are firm but not brown. Remove from pan to wire rack to cool.

Mix the 2 cups icing sugar and rum in a small mixing bowl; beat until smooth and drizzle over each cookie.

CHOCOLATE CHIP COOKIES

5 cups	flour
1 tsp	salt
2 cups	brown sugar
2 tsp	baking soda
1 cup	white sugar
2 cups	butter
4	eggs
3 tsp	vanilla extract
3 cups	chocolate chips

CREAM butter, brown sugar and white sugar until fluffy. Add the eggs and vanilla and beat well. Add the dry ingredients and chocolate chips and mix well. Drop by spoonfuls on greased cookie sheets and bake at 375°F for about 10–15 minutes.

SNOWBALLS

½ cup	butter
1½ cups	coconut
2 cups	sugar
1 tsp	vanilla extract
½ cup	milk
3⅓ cups	rolled oats
6 tbsp	cocoa

MIX well. Roll into balls. Roll in coconut. Put in freezer.

CINNAMON TREATS

2 cups	flour
1 tbsp	sugar
1 tbsp	baking powder
½ tsp	salt
½ cup	butter
¾ cup	milk

Filling

½ cup	pecans, ground
2 tsp	cinnamon
½ cup	packed brown sugar
1 tbsp	butter, melted

Glaze

¾ cup	sugar
4 tsp	milk
⅛ tsp	vanilla extract

MEASURE first four ingredients into large bowl. Cut in Butter until mixture is crumbly. Add milk, stir to form soft ball. Knead gently about 8 times on lightly floured surface. Pat or roll out into 10 × 15 inch rectangle.

To make filling, mix pecans, brown sugar, and cinnamon in small bowl. Brush dough with butter. Sprinkle with cinnamon mixture, keeping about ½ inch in from edges. Roll up from longside. Pinch seam to seal. Cut into 20 slices ¾ inch thick. Arrange on greased baking sheet placing about 1 inch apart. Bake in oven at 400°F for 12–14 minutes until lightly browned.

BANANA BONANZA COOKIES

1 cup	butter
1 cup	icing sugar
⅓ cup	bananas, mashed
½ tsp	vanilla extract
¼ tsp	salt
2⅔ cup	flour
½ cup	almonds, finely chopped
⅓ cup	cream cheese
1 cup	icing sugar
1 tbsp	maraschino cherries, very well drained & finely chopped

CREAM the butter and 1 cup of icing sugar together until fluffy. Add bananas, vanilla and salt beating well. Add flour and mix well.

STIR in the almonds, cover and chill for at least 1 hour.

FORM small balls of the dough, place on ungreased cookie sheet and flatten with bottom of a glass or cookie press which has been dipped in white sugar.

BAKE at 350°F for about 10 minutes or until just starting to turn golden. Cool. Beat together the cream cheese, 1 cup icing sugar and maraschino cherries. Put cookies together sandwich style with the icing.

BOILED RAISIN COOKIES

2 cups	raisins
1 cup	water
1 tsp	baking soda
1 cup	butter
1¾ cup	brown sugar
2	eggs
3 cups	flour
½ tsp	salt
2 tsp	cinnamon
½ tsp	nutmeg
1 tsp	vanilla extract

Boil raisins and water together for 5 minutes. Remove from heat and add soda. In a large bowl, cream the butter, sugar, eggs and vanilla.

Mix dry ingredients together and add to the creamed mixture along with the raisins.

Drop on greased cookie sheet and bake at 350°F for about 15 minutes or until done.

MAGIC CHIPIT BAR COOKIES

½ cup	butter
1½ cups	graham wafer crumbs
1 cup	chopped almonds and/or walnuts
1 cup	chocolate chips
1½ cups	coconut, shredded
1 can	sweetened condensed milk (300 ml)

MELT ½ cup butter in a 9 × 13 pan. Add 1½ cups graham wafer crumbs and press down firmly. In layers put 1 cup chopped nuts, 1 cup chocolate chips and 1½ cups of coconut on top of the crust. Drizzle 1 can of sweetened condensed milk over all and bake for 25 minutes at 350°F.

CHERRY SURPRISES

½ cup	butter, softened
1¾ cup	icing sugar
1 tsp	orange juice
1½ cups	medium coconut
3½ dozen	maraschino cherries, drained
1 cup	graham wafer crumbs

CREAM the butter, gradually beat in the icing sugar and orange juice. Add and mix in the coconut. Mixture will be quite soft. Wrap a small portion of the coconut mixture around a maraschino cherry and then roll in the graham crumbs. Chill.

CHOCOLATE SANDWICH COOKIES

½ cup	shortening
1 cup	sugar
1	egg
1 tsp	vanilla
1½ cup	flour
⅓ cup	cocoa powder
½ tsp	baking soda
½ tsp	salt
¼ cup	milk
1 tbsp	marshmallow cream

Cream shortening, sugar, egg and vanilla until light and fluffy. Combine flour, cocoa, baking soda and salt; add to the creamed mixture alternately with the milk until well combined.

Drop by teaspoonfuls onto a greased cookie sheet.

Bake at 375°F for about 12 minutes until just soft set (do not overbake). Cool 1 minute.

Remove from pans and cod completely on rack. Spread one cookie with about 1 tbsp of marshmallow cream and cover with another cookie. Repeat with remaining cookies and filling.

KRACKER JACK COOKIES

1 cup	butter
1 cup	brown sugar
1 cup	white sugar
2	eggs
2 tsp	vanilla extract
1½ cups	flour
1 tsp	baking powder
1 tsp	baking soda
2 cups	oatmeal
1 cup	coconut
2 cups	Rice Krispies
½ tsp	salt

CREAM butter and sugars. Beat eggs and vanilla and add to sugar mixture. Add flour, baking powder, baking soda and salt. Stir in the coconut and oatmeal.

MIX in the Rice Krispies. Place by spoonfuls on greased cookie sheet.

BAKE at 350°F for 10–15 minutes.

MARILYN'S OATMEAL COOKIES

1 cup	flour
1 tsp	baking soda
2½ cups	oatmeal
½ cup	shortening
½ cup	butter
1 cup	brown sugar
1	egg
¼ tsp	vanilla

CREAM shortening and butter. Add sugar, egg and vanilla. Beat till fluffy then add the dry ingredients. Drop onto greased cookie sheets. Make an indentation in the top of each cookie and fill the hole with jam of your choice. Bake at 375°F for 12–15 minutes.

MONSTER COOKIES

1 dozen	eggs
4½ cups	brown sugar
1 tbsp	vanilla extract
8 tsp	baking soda
6 cups	peanut butter
18 cups	oatmeal
1 pound	chocolate chips
1 pound	Smarties
1 pound	butter
2 cups	peanuts, chopped

COMBINE sugar, eggs, peanut butter and vanilla. Mix well. Add oatmeal, baking soda and butter. Combine well. Mix in chocolate chips, Smarties and peanuts. Drop by spoonfuls on greased cookie sheets. Bake at 350°F for 10–12 minutes.

COCOA PECAN KISSES

1 cup	butter, softened
⅔ cup	sugar
1 tsp	vanilla
1⅔ cup	flour
¼ cup	cocoa powder
1 cup	pecans, finely chopped
54	Hershey's Kisses, unwrapped
sprinkling	icing sugar

CREAM butter, sugar and vanilla in large bowl until light and fluffy. Combine the flour and cocoa; blend into the creamed mixture. Add pecans; beat until well blended.

CHILL dough for 1 hour or until firm enough to handle.

SHAPE a scant tbsp of dough around each chocolate kiss, covering completely. Place on an ungreased cookie sheet.

BAKE at 375°F for 10–12 minutes or until almost set. Cool slightly. Remove from cookie sheet; cool completely on rack and roll in icing sugar.

CRIMINAL DESSERTS

COCONUT FINGERS

½ cup	milk
½ cup	sugar
½ cup	butter
3 cups	fine oatmeal, grind till fairly fine
1 cup	sweetened coconut, fine

Mix everything together and spread on greased cookie sheet. Cut into fingers and freeze until stiff.

Melt 1 package of chocolate chips with a dab of butter on low heat; add ¼ block of Parowax (7–10 tbsp.) and stir until melted.

Dip fingers into the chocolate mixture with tongs. Put on wax paper and put in fridge to set.

COFFEE FINGERS

1 cup	butter
½ cup	icing sugar
2 cups	flour
¼ tsp	baking powder
½ tsp	vanilla extract
3 tbsp	butter
1 tsp	instant coffee powder
1½ tsp	hot water
1 cup	icing sugar

CREAM the 1 cup butter and ½ cup icing sugar together. Gradually stir in flour, baking powder and vanilla. Mix well. Put in cookie press and press out 1 inch lengths on ungreased cookie sheet.

BAKE in a 375°F oven for about 7 minutes until edges are just starting to brown. Don't overbake. Let cool completely on racks.

CREAM the 3 tbsp. butter until fluffy. Dissolve the instant coffee powder in the hot water and stir into the butter. Gradually beat in enough icing sugar to make filling of spreading consistency.

PRESS 2 cookies together with some filling. These can also be frozen.

David Bourne

Evolution happens all the time, for me the time it happens the most is at camp. At camp you evolve from just a kid to a higher person and it happens so suddenly that you can't even feel it happening 'til you're already on the ride home. My journey started about six years ago at Shawnigan Lake. When you start at camp you don't know where you are supposed to go so you stick with your cabin but as you grow and evolve you begin to branch out and become this very fun, eager, exited person who is bubbling with energy and joy.

The moments that I like most at camp are the ones I can't describe even if I thought about it all year I could never find the word. So at the very moment the registration forms come out I'm there with a pen because I know that I'm going to camp to make new friends and greet the old like I just came home from a long vacation.

When I think of camp it always gets summed up in the dance where we all are together to look back and just enjoy the last moments of the final night. As I'm standing there listening to "Alive" I start the week over in my head from the very moment I get there with the friendly hellos and the heart filled hugs. The next thing I think of is the water how it looks so inviting but is always so cold when you jump in. When I get to the beginning of the dance the song is over and I simply stand there yelling nothing special but it mixes well with the other noises going on around me.

When I leave camp the following morning I'm always the last to leave because I want to enjoy the final moment of camp. This way I can keep it in my heart for the rest of the year 'til the next time I get to see all those smiling faces.

David (left) and his friend.

Notes

Leave it to an airline to make a child's heart soar.

WestJet is proud to support children's charities across the country.

We extend our caring culture into Canadian communities with our WestJet Cares for Kids program. From once-in-a-lifetime vacations for the family of a sick child to helping reuniting missing children with their families, WestJet and our WestJet Cares for Kids partners are here to help.

WESTJET
CARES FOR **KIDS**

ENGAGE BOOKS™

FOR OTHER GREAT TITLES VISIT

WWW.ENGAGEBOOKS.CA

HOME OF

AD CLASSIC

GREATS

BC CLASSIC

LEGENDS

SF classic

HEROES

ENGAGE

LEADERS

JOURNEY INTO THE BOWELS OF THE EARTH
To a place where the White Rabbit could never take you!

ILLUSTRATED COLLECTORS EDITION
A.R. ROUMANIS EDITOR

JOURNEY TO THE CENTER OF THE EARTH

JULES VERNE

INTRODUCTION BY MARK RICH

ISBN: 9781926606194

50 ILLUSTRATIONS

BIOGRAPHY ON VERNE

INTRODUCTION BY MARK RICH

Available at
WWW.SFCLASSICBOOKS.COM

BREAST CANCER JOURNAL
All proceeds benefit the Weekend to End Breast Cancer

ISBN: 9781926606224
108 LINED PAGES
Available at
WWW.ENGAGEBOOKS.CA

AD CLASSIC

FOR OTHER GREAT TITLES VISIT

WWW.ADCLASSICBOOKS.COM

The greats from the past two thousand years

DANIEL DEFOE
Robinson Crusoe

ISBN: 9781926606163

JULES VERNE
A Journey to the Center of the Earth

ISBN: 9780980921038

LEWIS CARROLL
Alice's Adventures in Wonderland

ISBN: 9780980921090

LEWIS CARROLL
Through the Looking-Glass

ISBN: 9781926606170

AD CLASSIC

FOR OTHER GREAT TITLES VISIT

WWW.ADCLASSICBOOKS.COM

The greats from the past two thousand years

MARY SHELLEY
Frankenstein

ISBN: 9780980921045

H.G. Wells
THE WAR OF THE WORLDS

ISBN: 9780980921014

ELIZABETH GASKELL
Cranford

ISBN: 9780980921021

NICCOLÒ MACHIAVELLI
The Prince

ISBN: 9780980921052

BC CLASSIC

FOR OTHER GREAT TITLES VISIT

WWW.BCCLASSICBOOKS.COM

Legends of Old

Year	Title	Author	ISBN
c.250 BC	The Argonautica: Jason and the Golden Fleece	Apollonius of Rhodes	9781926606149
c.330 BC	Politics	Aristotle	9781926606040
c.350 BC	Nicomachean Ethics	Aristotle	9781926606057
c.360 BC	Republic	Plato	9781926606064
c.385 BC	Symposium	Plato	9781926606071
c.411 BC	Lysistrata	Aristophanes	9781926606088
c.429 BC / c.406 BC / c.442 BC	The Oedipus Plays: Oedipus The King, Oedipus at Colonus, Antigone	Sophocles	9781926606095
c.479 BC	The Analects of Confucius	Confucius	9781926606101
c.590 BC	Aesop's Fables	Aesop	9781926606118
c.725 BC	Odyssey	Homer	9781926606125
c.750 BC	Iliad	Homer	9781926606132

Some titles have not yet been released. Visit www.bcclassicbooks.com for the latest update.

AD CLASSIC

FOR OTHER GREAT TITLES VISIT

WWW.ADCLASSICBOOKS.COM

The greats from the past two thousand years

Year	Title	Author	ISBN
1902 AD	Heart of Darkness	Joseph Conrad	9781926606002
1899 AD	The Awakening	Kate Chopin	9781926606026
1898 AD	War of the Worlds	H.G. Wells	9780980921014
1895 AD	The Time Machine	H.G. Wells	9780980921083
1883 AD	Treasure Island	Robert Louis Stevenson	9781926606187
1871 AD	Through the Looking-Glass	Lewis Carroll	9781926606170
1865 AD	Alice's Adventures in Wonderland	Lewis Carroll	9780980921090
1864 AD	A Journey to the Center of the Earth	Jules Verne	9780980921038
1853 AD	Cranford	Elizabeth Gaskell	9780980921021
1848 AD	The Communist Manifesto	Karl Marx	9780980921076
1843 AD	A Christmas Carol	Charles Dickens	9780980921069
1818 AD	Frankenstein	Mary Shelley	9780980921045
1759 AD	Candide	Voltaire	9781926606019
1719 AD	Robinson Crusoe	Daniel Defoe	9781926606163
1532 AD	The Prince	Niccolò Machiavelli	9780980921052
c.850 AD	Beowulf	Anonymous	9781926606033

Printed in the United States
153196LV00003B/28/P